THE AIR FRYER COOK BOOK

a simple handbook

Contents

1

An Introduction to your Air Fryer

An air fryer is a popular kitchen appliance that allows you to cook your favorite fried foods in a healthier way. It works by circulating hot air around the food, which creates a crispy and crunchy texture similar to that of deep-fried foods, but without the added oil.

Air fryers are becoming increasingly popular because they are a healthier alternative to deep frying, which requires a lot of oil and can lead to excess calories and fat in your diet. With an air fryer, you can enjoy your favorite fried foods, such as chicken wings, french fries, and onion rings, with less oil, making them a better option for your health.

Not only are air fryers healthier, they are also incredibly versatile. They can be used to cook a variety of foods, from vegetables and seafood to meat and desserts. In fact, many air fryer recipes are quick and easy to prepare, making them perfect for busy weeknights or for those who want to enjoy their favorite foods without spending too much time in the kitchen.

In addition to being a healthier option, air fryers are also environmentally friendly, as they use less oil and energy than traditional deep fryers. This means that not only are you making a healthier choice for yourself, you are also contributing to a greener planet.

Air fryers are a great addition to any kitchen, whether you are health-conscious or just love fried foods. With their versatility, ease of use, and healthier cooking methods, air fryers are sure to become a staple in many households.

How do they work?

Air fryers work by circulating hot air around the food, creating a crispy and crunchy texture similar to deep-fried foods, but with less oil. The process of cooking in an air fryer is simple and efficient, and it can be broken down into three basic steps: heating, circulating, and cooking.

1.   Heating The heating element in the air fryer heats the air inside the fryer to a high temperature, usually between 300°F and 400°F (150°C and 200°C). The heating element is typically located at the top of the air fryer and is responsible for heating the air that will cook the food.

2.   Circulating The hot air is then circulated around the food using a fan, which is located above the heating element. The fan helps to distribute the hot air evenly throughout the fryer, ensuring that the food is cooked evenly and thoroughly.

3.   Cooking As the hot air circulates around the food, it cooks the food by creating a crispy and crunchy texture on the outside, while keeping the inside moist and tender. The cooking time for each recipe may vary depending on the type of food and the quantity being cooked.

Air fryers typically have a basket or tray where the food is placed. The basket or tray is designed with perforations, allowing the hot air to flow through and cook the food evenly. Some air fryers also come with accessories, such as baking pans, racks, or skewers, which can be used to cook a variety of foods.

One of the key benefits of using an air fryer is that it requires very little oil compared to traditional deep frying. In fact, most air fryer recipes require only a small amount of oil, or no oil at all, making them a healthier option for those who want to enjoy fried foods without the added calories and fat.

Air fryers work by using hot air to cook food, creating a healthier and more efficient alternative to traditional deep frying.

Tips for using an Air fryer

Preheat the air fryer:

While air fryers don't require preheating like traditional ovens, it's still a good idea to preheat the air fryer for a few minutes before adding your food. This will ensure that the air fryer is hot enough to cook your food evenly and thoroughly.

Don't overcrowd the basket:

To ensure that your food cooks evenly, make sure not to overcrowd the basket. Leave some space between the food items to allow the hot air to circulate freely.

Use a light coating of oil:

While air fryers require less oil than traditional frying methods, using a light coating of oil can help to create a crispy texture on your food. Use a spray bottle or a pastry brush to apply a light coat of oil to your food.

Shake the basket:

To ensure even cooking, shake the basket halfway through cooking to flip and redistribute the food.

Monitor the cooking time:

Different foods may require different cooking times in an air fryer, so it's important to monitor the cooking time and adjust as needed. Use a meat thermometer to ensure that meat is cooked to the appropriate temperature.

Clean the air fryer regularly:

Regularly cleaning the air fryer will help to prevent buildup of food particles and oil, which can affect the performance of the appliance. Make sure to follow the manufacturer's instructions for cleaning and maintenance.

Experiment with different recipes:

Air fryers are versatile appliances that can be used to cook a variety of foods. Experiment with different recipes and cooking techniques to find what works best for you and your family.

By following these tips, you can ensure that your air fryer performs at its best and that your food comes out delicious and crispy every time.

2

Appetisers & Snacks

Chicken Wings

Ingredients:

- ➲ 500 g chicken wings
- ➲ 1 teaspoon baking powder
- ➲ 1/2 teaspoon salt
- ➲ 1/2 teaspoon garlic powder
- ➲ 1/2 teaspoon paprika
- ➲ 1/4 teaspoon black pepper

Instructions:

1. Preheat your air fryer to 200°C/400°F.

2. Rinse the chicken wings under cold running water and pat dry with paper towels.

3. In a small bowl, mix together the baking powder, salt, garlic powder, paprika, and black pepper.

4. Add the chicken wings to a large bowl and sprinkle the spice mixture over them, making sure to coat them evenly.

5. Place the chicken wings in the air fryer basket, making sure they are not touching each other. You may need to cook the wings in batches depending on the size of your air fryer.

6. Cook the wings for 10 minutes.

7. After 10 minutes, remove the air fryer basket and flip the wings over using a pair of tongs.

8. Place the basket back in the air fryer and cook for another 10-12 minutes or until the wings are golden brown and crispy.

9. Once done, remove the wings from the air fryer and let them rest for a couple of minutes before serving.

Onion Rings

Ingredients:

- ⮐ 1 large onion, sliced into rings
- ⮐ 1 cup all-purpose flour
- ⮐ 1 teaspoon salt
- ⮐ 1/2 teaspoon black pepper
- ⮐ 2 eggs
- ⮐ 1 cup breadcrumbs

Instructions:

1. Preheat your air fryer to 200°C/400°F.

2. In a bowl, mix together the flour, salt, and black pepper.

3. In another bowl, beat the eggs.

4. Put the breadcrumbs in a third bowl.

5. Dip each onion ring into the flour mixture, then into the egg mixture, and finally into the breadcrumbs, making sure each ring is fully coated

6.   Place the onion rings in the air fryer basket, making sure they are not touching each other.

7.   Cook for 8-10 minutes or until the onion rings are golden brown and crispy.

8.   Serve immediately with your favourite dipping sauce.

French Fries

Ingredients:

- ⮑ 2 large potatoes, peeled and cut into thin fries
- ⮑ 2 tablespoons vegetable oil
- ⮑ 1 teaspoon salt
- ⮑ 1/2 teaspoon garlic powder
- ⮑ 1/2 teaspoon paprika

Instructions:

1. Preheat your air fryer to 200°C/400°F.

2. In a bowl, mix together the vegetable oil, salt, garlic powder, and paprika.

3. Add the potato fries to the bowl and toss to coat them evenly in the oil mixture.

4. Place the fries in the air fryer basket, making sure they are not touching each other.

5. Cook for 12-15 minutes or until the fries are golden brown and crispy.

6. Serve immediately with ketchup or your favourite dipping sauce.

Mozzarella Sticks

Ingredients:

- ➲ 8 mozzarella sticks

- ➲ 1/2 cup all-purpose flour

- ➲ 2 eggs, beaten

- ➲ 1 cup breadcrumbs

- ➲ 1 teaspoon dried oregano

- ➲ 1/2 teaspoon garlic powder

- ➲ 1/4 teaspoon salt

- ➲ Marinara sauce for dipping

Instructions:

1. Preheat your air fryer to 200°C/400°F.

2. Cut the mozzarella sticks in half lengthwise.

3. In a bowl, mix together the breadcrumbs, dried oregano, garlic powder, and salt.

4. Dip each mozzarella stick half in the flour, then in the beaten egg, and finally in the breadcrumb mixture, making sure each stick is fully coated.

5. Place the mozzarella sticks in the air fryer basket, making sure they are not touching each other.

6. Cook for 6-8 minutes or until the mozzarella sticks are golden brown and crispy.

7. Serve immediately with marinara sauce for dipping.

Chicken Tenders

Ingredients:

- ⮁ 500 g chicken tenders
- ⮁ 1 cup plain flour
- ⮁ 2 eggs, beaten
- ⮁ 1 cup breadcrumbs
- ⮁ 1/2 teaspoon salt
- ⮁ 1/4 teaspoon black pepper
- ⮁ 1/4 teaspoon garlic powder
- ⮁ BBQ sauce for dipping

Instructions:

1. Preheat your air fryer to 200°C/400°F.

2. In a bowl, mix together the breadcrumbs, salt, black pepper, and garlic powder.

3. Dip each chicken tender in the flour, then in the beaten egg, and finally in the breadcrumb mixture, making sure each tender is fully coated.

4. Place the chicken tenders in the air fryer basket, making sure they are not touching each other.

5. Cook for 10-12 minutes or until the chicken tenders are golden brown and crispy.

6. Serve immediately with BBQ sauce for dipping.

3

Main Meals

Air Fryer Roast Chicken

Ingredients:

- ➲ 1 whole chicken
- ➲ 2 tablespoons olive oil
- ➲ 1 tablespoon salt
- ➲ 1/2 tablespoon black pepper
- ➲ 1 tablespoon garlic powder
- ➲ 1 tablespoon dried thyme

Instructions:

1. Preheat your air fryer to 180°C/350°F.

2. Rinse the chicken and pat dry with paper towels.

3. In a small bowl, mix together the olive oil, salt, black pepper, garlic powder, and thyme.

4. Rub the mixture all over the chicken, including inside the cavity.

5. Place the chicken in the air fryer basket, breast side up.

6. Cook for 30 minutes, then flip the chicken over and cook for another 30 minutes or until the internal temperature of the chicken reaches 75°C/165°F.

7. Let the chicken rest for 10 minutes before carving and serving.

Fish and Chips

Ingredients:

- 2 fillets of white fish, such as cod or haddock
- 1/2 cup all-purpose flour
- 1 teaspoon salt
- 1/2 teaspoon black pepper
- 1 egg, beaten
- 1 cup breadcrumbs
- 2 tablespoons vegetable oil
- 2 large potatoes, peeled and cut into thin fries
- Salt and pepper to taste

Instructions:

1. Preheat your air fryer to 200°C/400°F.

2. In a bowl, mix together the flour, salt, and black pepper.

3. In another bowl, beat the egg.

4.   Put the breadcrumbs in a third bowl.

5.   Dip each fish fillet into the flour mixture, then into the beaten egg, and finally into the breadcrumbs, making sure each fillet is fully coated.

6.   Place the fish fillets in the air fryer basket, making sure they are not touching each other.

7.   Cook for 10-12 minutes or until the fish is golden brown and crispy.

8.   In a separate bowl, mix together the vegetable oil, salt, and pepper.

9.   Toss the potato fries in the oil mixture and place them in the air fryer basket, making sure they are not touching each other.

10. Cook for 12-15 minutes or until the fries are golden brown and crispy.

11. Serve the fish and chips immediately with tartar sauce or your favourite dipping sauce.

Air Fryer Pork Chops

Ingredients:

- ⊃ 4 pork chops
- ⊃ 1 teaspoon salt
- ⊃ 1/2 teaspoon black pepper
- ⊃ 1 teaspoon garlic powder
- ⊃ 1 teaspoon dried thyme
- ⊃ 1 tablespoon olive oil

Instructions:

1. Preheat your air fryer to 200°C/400°F.

2. Season the pork chops with salt, black pepper, garlic powder, and dried thyme on both sides.

3. Brush the pork chops with olive oil on both sides.

4. Place the pork chops in the air fryer basket, making sure they are not touching each other.

5. Cook for 10-12 minutes or until the internal temperature of the pork chops reaches 70°C/160°F.

6. Let the pork chops rest for 5 minutes before serving.

Air Fryer Steak

Ingredients:

- ➲ 2 steaks, about 8 ounces each

- ➲ 1 teaspoon salt

- ➲ 1/2 teaspoon black pepper

- ➲ 1/2 teaspoon garlic powder

- ➲ 1 tablespoon olive oil

Instructions:

1. Preheat your air fryer to 200°C/400°F.

2. Season the steaks with salt, black pepper, and garlic powder on both sides.

3. Brush the steaks with olive oil on both sides.

4. Place the steaks in the air fryer basket, making sure they are not touching each other.

5. Cook for 6-8 minutes for medium-rare, 8-10 minutes for medium, or 10-12 minutes for well-done, flipping the steaks halfway through.

6. Let the steaks rest for 5 minutes before serving.

Air Fryer Vegetables

Ingredients:

- 500 g mixed vegetables, such as broccoli, carrots, and cauliflower

- 1 tablespoon olive oil

- 1/2 teaspoon salt

- 1/4 teaspoon black pepper

- 1/2 teaspoon garlic powder

- 1/2 teaspoon dried thyme

Instructions:

1. Preheat your air fryer to 200°C/400°F.

2. Cut the vegetables into bite-sized pieces.

3. In a bowl, mix together the olive oil, salt, black pepper, garlic powder, and dried thyme.

4. Add the vegetables to the bowl and toss to coat.

5. Place the vegetables in the air fryer basket, making sure they are not touching each other.

6. Cook for 10-12 minutes or until the vegetables are tender and lightly browned.

7. Serve the vegetables immediately as a side dish or as a topping for salads or bowls.

4

Breakfast & Brunch

Air Fryer Breakfast Hash

Ingredients:

- 500 g potatoes, peeled and diced

- 1/2 onion, diced

- 1 red bell pepper, diced

- 2 tablespoons olive oil

- 1 teaspoon garlic powder

- 1 teaspoon paprika

- 1/2 teaspoon salt

- 1/4 teaspoon black pepper

- 4 eggs

Instructions:

1. Preheat your air fryer to 200°C/400°F.

2. In a bowl, mix together the potatoes, onion, red bell pepper, olive oil, garlic powder, paprika, salt, and black pepper.

3. Transfer the mixture to the air fryer basket.

4. Cook for 15-20 minutes or until the potatoes are golden brown and crispy.

5. Make 4 wells in the hash and crack an egg into each well.

6. Cook for an additional 5-8 minutes or until the eggs are cooked to your liking.

7. Serve the breakfast hash immediately.

Breakfast Sandwiches

Ingredients:

- ⮐ 4 English muffins, split and toasted

- ⮐ 4 slices bacon

- ⮐ 4 eggs

- ⮐ 4 slices cheddar cheese

- ⮐ Salt and pepper to taste

Instructions:

1. Preheat your air fryer to 180°C/350°F.

2. Place the bacon in the air fryer basket and cook for 3-5 minutes or until heated through.

3. Crack an egg into each well of a silicone egg mould and season with salt and pepper.

4. Place the egg mould in the air fryer basket and cook for 5-7 minutes or until the eggs are cooked to your liking.

5. Assemble the breakfast sandwiches by placing a slice of cheese on the bottom half of each English muffin, followed by the bacon (or ham), and finally the cooked egg.

6. Top with the other half of the English muffin and serve immediately.

Omelettes

Ingredients:

- 3 eggs
- 1/4 cup milk
- Salt and pepper to taste
- 1/2 cup shredded cheddar cheese
- 1/4 cup diced ham or cooked bacon
- 1/4 cup diced bell peppers
- 1/4 cup diced onions

Instructions:

1. Preheat your air fryer to 180°C/350°F.

2. In a bowl, whisk together the eggs, milk, salt, and pepper.

3. Fold in the shredded cheddar cheese, diced ham or cooked bacon, diced bell peppers, and diced onions.

4. Pour the egg mixture into a greased air fryer-safe baking dish or ramekin.

5. Place the baking dish or ramekin in the air fryer basket.

6. Cook for 10-12

7. minutes or until the omelette is set and cooked through.

8. Remove the baking dish or ramekin from the air fryer and let it cool for a few minutes.

9. Use a spatula to loosen the edges of the omelette and slide it onto a plate.

10. Serve immediately.

Quiche

Ingredients:

- ⮑ 1 refrigerated pie crust

- ⮑ 6 eggs

- ⮑ 1 cup milk

- ⮑ 1/2 cup shredded cheddar cheese

- ⮑ 1/2 cup diced ham or cooked bacon

- ⮑ 1/4 cup diced onions

- ⮑ 1/4 cup diced bell peppers

- ⮑ Salt and pepper to taste

Instructions:

1. Preheat your air fryer to 180°C/350°F.

2. Unroll the pie crust and place it in a greased air fryer-safe baking dish.

3. In a bowl, whisk together the eggs, milk, salt, and pepper.

4. Fold in the shredded cheddar cheese, diced ham or cooked bacon, diced onions, and diced bell peppers.

5. Pour the egg mixture into the pie crust.

6. Place the baking dish in the air fryer basket.

7. Cook for 20-25 minutes or until the quiche is set and cooked through.

8. Remove the baking dish from the air fryer and let it cool for a few minutes.

9. Use a knife to cut the quiche into slices and serve immediately.

5

Deserts

Air Fryer Apple Crisps

Ingredients:

- ➲ 2 medium-sized apples

- ➲ 1 teaspoon ground cinnamon

- ➲ 1 tablespoon granulated sugar

Instructions:

1. Preheat your air fryer to 120°C/250°F.

2. Slice the apples thinly using a mandoline or a sharp knife.

3. In a small bowl, mix together the cinnamon and sugar.

4. Place the sliced apples in a single layer in the air fryer basket.

5. Sprinkle the cinnamon sugar mixture over the sliced apples.

6. Cook the apple chips in the air fryer for 10-12 minutes or until they are crispy and golden brown.

7. Remove the apple crisps from the air fryer and let them cool completely before serving.

Donuts

Ingredients:

- ➲ 250g plain flour
- ➲ 75g caster sugar
- ➲ 2 tsp baking powder
- ➲ 1/4 tsp salt
- ➲ 125ml milk
- ➲ 2 large eggs, lightly beaten
- ➲ 2 tbsp unsalted butter, melted
- ➲ 1 tsp vanilla extract
- ➲ 2-3 tbsp vegetable oil
- ➲ Additional caster sugar, for dusting

Instructions:

1. In a large mixing bowl, whisk together the flour, caster sugar, baking powder, and salt until well combined.

2. In a separate bowl, whisk together the milk, eggs, melted butter, and vanilla extract.

3. Pour the wet ingredients into the dry ingredients and stir until just combined.

4. Cover the bowl with a damp cloth and let the dough rest for 10 minutes.

5. Preheat your air fryer to 180°C/360°F.

6. Lightly dust your work surface with flour and roll out the dough to a thickness of about 1 cm.

7. Using a donut cutter, cut out as many donuts as possible.

8. Brush the donuts with vegetable oil on both sides.

9. Place the donuts in the air fryer basket, making sure they are not touching each other.

10. Air fry the donuts for 5-6 minutes, flipping them halfway through the cooking time, until they are golden brown.

11. Remove the donuts from the air fryer basket and let them cool for a few minutes.

12. While the donuts are still warm, dust them with caster sugar.

13. Serve and enjoy your freshly made air fryer donuts!

Air Fryer Brownies

Ingredients:

- 1/2 cup unsalted butter, melted
- 1 cup granulated sugar
- 1/2 cup unsweetened cocoa powder
- 1/2 teaspoon salt
- 2 large eggs
- 1 teaspoon vanilla extract
- 1/2 cup all-purpose flour
- 1/4 cup chocolate chips

Instructions:

1. Preheat your air fryer to 175°C/350°F.

2. In a large bowl, whisk together the melted butter, sugar, cocoa powder, and salt.

3. Add the eggs and vanilla extract to the bowl and whisk until well combined.

4. Fold in the flour and chocolate chips.

5. Pour the brownie batter into a greased air fryer-safe baking dish.

6. Place the baking dish in the air fryer basket and cook the brownies for 12-15 minutes or until a toothpick inserted in the center comes out clean.

7. Remove the baking dish from the air fryer and let the brownies cool for a few minutes before slicing and serving.

Air Fryer Chocolate Chip Cookies

Ingredients:

- ➲ 1/2 cup unsalted butter, at room temperature
- ➲ 1/2 cup granulated sugar
- ➲ 1/2 cup brown sugar
- ➲ 1 large egg
- ➲ 1 teaspoon vanilla extract
- ➲ 1 1/2 cups plain flour
- ➲ 1/2 teaspoon baking soda
- ➲ 1/4 teaspoon salt
- ➲ 1 cup chocolate chips

Instructions:

1. Preheat your air fryer to 175°C/350°F.

2. In a large bowl, cream together the butter, granulated sugar, and brown sugar until light and fluffy.

3. Beat in the egg and vanilla extract until well combined.

4. In a separate bowl, whisk together the flour, baking soda, and salt.

5. Gradually mix the dry ingredients into the butter mixture until just combined.

6. Fold in the chocolate chips.

7. Drop spoonfuls of the cookie dough onto a greased air fryer basket, leaving space between each cookie.

8. Cook the cookies in the air fryer for 8-10 minutes or until they are golden brown and set.

9. Remove the cookies from the air fryer and let them cool for a few minutes before serving.

Air Fryer Banana Bread

Ingredients:

- 2 ripe bananas, mashed
- 1/3 cup unsalted butter, melted
- 1/2 cup granulated sugar
- 1 large egg
- 1 teaspoon vanilla extract
- 1 1/2 cups all-purpose flour
- 1/2 teaspoon baking soda
- 1/4 teaspoon salt

Instructions:

1. Preheat your air fryer to 160°C/320°F.

2. In a large bowl, mix together the mashed bananas, melted butter, granulated sugar, egg, and vanilla extract.

3. In a separate bowl, whisk together the flour, baking soda, and salt.

4.   Gradually mix the dry ingredients into the banana mixture until just combined.

5.   Pour the banana bread batter into a greased air fryer-safe baking dish.

6.   Place the baking dish in the air fryer basket and cook the banana bread for 25-30 minutes or until a toothpick inserted in the center comes out clean.

7.   Remove the baking dish from the air fryer and let the banana bread cool for a few minutes before slicing and serving.

Molten Lava Cake

Ingredients:

- 100g dark chocolate

- 50g unsalted butter, plus extra for greasing

- 2 large eggs

- 50g caster sugar

- 1 tsp vanilla extract

- 30g plain flour

- Pinch of salt

Instructions:

1. Preheat your air fryer to 180°C/360°F.

2. Grease two ramekins with butter.

3. Melt the chocolate and butter together in a heatproof bowl set over a pan of simmering water. Stir until smooth and remove from the heat.

4. In a separate bowl, whisk together the eggs, caster sugar, and vanilla extract until light and frothy.

5. Pour the melted chocolate mixture into the egg mixture and whisk until well combined.

6. Sift in the flour and salt and fold in gently until just combined.

7. Divide the mixture between the two prepared ramekins.

8. Place the ramekins in the air fryer basket and air fry for 7-8 minutes, until the cakes are set around the edges but still gooey in the middle.

9. Remove the ramekins from the air fryer basket and let them cool for a few minutes.

10. Run a knife around the edges of the ramekins and turn out the cakes onto serving plates.

11. Serve your delicious Air Fryer Molten Lava Cakes warm, garnished with a sprinkle of icing sugar and a scoop of vanilla ice cream, if desired.

6

Kids favourites

Chicken Nuggets

Ingredients:

- 500 g boneless, skinless chicken breasts, cut into bite-sized pieces

- 1/2 cup all-purpose flour

- 1 teaspoon paprika

- 1 teaspoon garlic powder

- 1/2 teaspoon salt

- 1/4 teaspoon black pepper

- 2 large eggs, beaten

- 1 1/2 cups panko breadcrumbs

- Cooking spray

Instructions:

1. Preheat your air fryer to 190°C/375°F.

2. In a bowl, mix together the flour, paprika, garlic powder, salt, and black pepper.

3. In a separate bowl, beat the eggs.

4. Place the panko breadcrumbs in a third bowl.

5. Dip each chicken piece into the flour mixture, then the beaten eggs, and finally the panko breadcrumbs, pressing the breadcrumbs onto the chicken to coat it well.

6. Place the breaded chicken nuggets in a single layer in the air fryer basket.

7. Spray the nuggets with cooking spray to help them brown.

8. Cook the chicken nuggets for 10-12 minutes, flipping them halfway through, until they are golden brown and cooked through.

9. Serve the chicken nuggets with your favorite dipping sauce.

Air Fryer Pizza

Ingredients:

- 1 pre-made pizza crust or homemade pizza dough
- 1/2 cup pizza sauce
- 1 cup shredded mozzarella cheese
- 1/4 cup grated Parmesan cheese
- Toppings of your choice

Instructions:

1. Preheat your air fryer to 200°C/400°F.

2. Roll out your pizza dough or spread the pre-made crust with pizza sauce.

3. Sprinkle the shredded mozzarella cheese and grated Parmesan cheese over the pizza.

4. Add your desired toppings.

5. Place the pizza in the air fryer basket and cook for 8-10 minutes or until the cheese is melted and bubbly and the crust is golden brown.

6. Remove the pizza from the air fryer and let it cool for a few minutes before slicing and serving.

Homemade Fish Sticks

Ingredients:

- 500 g cod or other white fish, cut into strips

- 1/2 cup all-purpose flour

- 1/2 teaspoon garlic powder

- 1/2 teaspoon paprika

- 1/4 teaspoon salt

- 2 large eggs, beaten

- 1 1/2 cups panko breadcrumbs

- Cooking spray

Instructions:

1. Preheat your air fryer to 190°C/375°F.

2. In a bowl, mix together the flour, garlic powder, paprika, and salt.

3. In a separate bowl, beat the eggs.

4. Place the panko breadcrumbs in a third bowl.

5. Dip each fish strip into the flour mixture, then the beaten eggs, and finally the panko breadcrumbs, pressing the breadcrumbs onto the fish to coat it well.

6. Place the breaded fish sticks in a single layer in the air fryer basket.

7. Spray the fish sticks with cooking spray to help them brown.

8. Cook the fish sticks for 10-12 minutes, flipping them halfway through, until they are golden brown and cooked through.

9. Serve the fish sticks with tartar sauce or ketchup.

Cheesy Quesadillas

Ingredients:

- ➲ 4 flour tortillas

- ➲ 1 cup shredded cheddar cheese

- ➲ 1/2 cup black beans, rinsed and drained

- ➲ 1/2 cup corn kernels

- ➲ 1/4 cup diced red onion

- ➲ 1/4 cup chopped fresh cilantro

- ➲ Cooking spray

Instructions:

1. Preheat your air fryer to 190°C/375°F.

2. 2. Place one tortilla on a flat surface and sprinkle half of the cheese over one half of the tortilla.

3. Add the black beans, corn, red onion, and cilantro on top of the cheese.

4. Sprinkle the remaining cheese on top of the toppings.

THE AIR FRYER COOK BOOK

5. Fold the other half of the tortilla over the filling to create a half-moon shape.

6. Spray the air fryer basket with cooking spray.

7. Place the quesadilla in the air fryer basket and cook for 5-7 minutes, flipping halfway through, until the cheese is melted and the tortilla is crispy.

8. Remove the quesadilla from the air fryer and let it cool for a minute before slicing and serving.

Mini Corn Dogs

Ingredients:

- 8 hot dogs, cut into bite-sized pieces

- 1/2 cup all-purpose flour

- 1/2 cup cornmeal

- 2 tablespoons sugar

- 2 teaspoons baking powder

- 1/4 teaspoon salt

- 1/2 cup milk

- 1 large egg

- Cooking spray

Instructions:

1. Preheat your air fryer to 190°C/375°F.

2. In a bowl, mix together the flour, cornmeal, sugar, baking powder, and salt.

3. In a separate bowl, whisk together the milk and egg.

4. Add the wet ingredients to the dry ingredients and stir until just combined.

5. Dip each hot dog piece into the batter to coat it well.

6. Place the corn dogs in a single layer in the air fryer basket.

7. Spray the corn dogs with cooking spray to help them brown.

8. Cook the corn dogs for 8-10 minutes, flipping them halfway through, until they are golden brown and cooked through.

9. Serve the mini corn dogs with ketchup or mustard for dipping.

Calories Controlled Recipes

7

Air Fryer Turkey Burgers

Ingredients:

- ➲ 500 g ground turkey
- ➲ 1/2 teaspoon salt
- ➲ 1/4 teaspoon black pepper
- ➲ 1/2 teaspoon garlic powder
- ➲ 1/2 teaspoon onion powder
- ➲ 1 tablespoon Worcestershire sauce
- ➲ Cooking spray

Instructions:

1. Preheat your air fryer to 190°C/375°F.

2. In a bowl, mix together the ground turkey, salt, black pepper, garlic powder, onion powder, and Worcestershire sauce until well combined.

3. Divide the mixture into 4 equal portions and shape each portion into a patty.

4. Spray the air fryer basket with cooking spray.

5. Place the turkey burgers in the air fryer basket and cook for 10-12 minutes, flipping halfway through, until they are cooked through.

6. Serve the turkey burgers with your favourite toppings, such as lettuce, tomato, and avocado.

Baked Sweet Potato Fries

Ingredients:

- ➲ 2 medium sweet potatoes, peeled and cut into thin fries
- ➲ 1 tablespoon cornstarch
- ➲ 1/2 teaspoon salt
- ➲ 1/4 teaspoon black pepper
- ➲ 1/2 teaspoon paprika
- ➲ Cooking spray

Instructions:

1. Preheat your air fryer to 190°C/375°F.

2. In a bowl, toss the sweet potato fries with the cornstarch, salt, black pepper, and paprika until well coated.

3. Spray the air fryer basket with cooking spray.

4. Place the sweet potato fries in the air fryer basket in a single layer.

5. Cook the sweet potato fries for 15-18 minutes, shaking the basket occasionally, until they are crispy and tender.

6. Serve the sweet potato fries as a side dish or snack.

Air Fryer Chicken Breast

Ingredients:

- 2 boneless, skinless chicken breasts
- 1/2 teaspoon salt
- 1/4 teaspoon black pepper
- 1/2 teaspoon garlic powder
- 1/2 teaspoon onion powder
- Cooking spray

Instructions:

1. Preheat your air fryer to 190°C/375°F.

2. Season the chicken breasts with the salt, black pepper, garlic powder, and onion powder.

3. Spray the air fryer basket with cooking spray.

4. Place the chicken breasts in the air fryer basket and cook for 10-12 minutes, flipping halfway through, until they are cooked through and the internal temperature reaches 75°C/165°F.

5. Let the chicken breasts rest for a few minutes before slicing and serving.

Air Fryer Tofu Nuggets

Ingredients:

- ⮕ 1 block firm tofu, pressed and cut into bite-sized pieces
- ⮕ 1/4 cup all-purpose flour
- ⮕ 1/4 teaspoon salt
- ⮕ 1/4 teaspoon black pepper
- ⮕ 1/4 teaspoon garlic powder
- ⮕ 1/4 teaspoon onion powder
- ⮕ 1/2 cup panko breadcrumbs
- ⮕ 1 egg, beaten
- ⮕ Cooking spray

Instructions:

1. Preheat your air fryer to 190°C/375°F.

2. In a bowl, mix together the flour, salt, black pepper, garlic powder, and onion powder.

3. In a separate bowl, beat the egg.

4. In a third bowl, place the panko breadcrumbs.

5. Dip each piece of tofu into the flour mixture, shaking off any excess.

6. Dip the tofu into the beaten egg, then coat it with the panko breadcrumbs.

7. Spray the air fryer basket with cooking spray.

8. Place the tofu nuggets in the air fryer basket in a single layer.

9. Cook the tofu nuggets for 8-10 minutes, flipping halfway through, until they are crispy and golden brown. 10. Serve the tofu nuggets with your favourite dipping sauce.

Grilled Cheese Sandwich

Ingredients:

- ⮑ 2 slices whole wheat bread
- ⮑ 1/4 cup shredded cheddar cheese
- ⮑ 1/4 cup shredded mozzarella cheese
- ⮑ 1 tablespoon butter

Instructions:

1. Preheat your air fryer to 190°C/375°F.
2. Mix together the cheddar cheese and mozzarella cheese in a bowl.
3. Butter one side of each slice of bread.
4. Place one slice of bread, butter side down, in the air fryer basket.
5. Sprinkle half of the cheese mixture on top of the bread slice.
6. Place the other slice of bread, butter side up, on top of the cheese.
7. Cook the grilled cheese sandwich for 5-7 minutes, flipping halfway through, until the bread is crispy and the cheese is melted.
8. Serve the grilled cheese sandwich hot.

Note: For a lower calorie version, use reduced-fat cheese and whole grain bread.

8

Date Night Recipies

Air Fryer Shrimp Scampi

Ingredients:

- ➲ 500 g large shrimp, peeled and deveined
- ➲ 4 tablespoons butter
- ➲ 4 cloves garlic, minced
- ➲ 1/4 teaspoon red pepper flakes
- ➲ 2 tablespoons fresh lemon juice
- ➲ Salt and black pepper, to taste
- ➲ Fresh parsley, chopped

Instructions:

1. Preheat your air fryer to 190°C/375°F.

2. In a skillet over medium heat, melt the butter. Add garlic and red pepper flakes and cook for 1-2 minutes.

3. Add shrimp to the skillet and cook for 2-3 minutes until pink and cooked through.

4. Remove from heat and stir in the lemon juice, salt, and black pepper.

5. Place the shrimp in the air fryer basket and cook for 3-5 minutes until crispy and golden.

6. Sprinkle with chopped parsley and serve hot.

Garlic Butter Steak Bites

Ingredients:

- ⮑ 500 g sirloin steak, cut into bite-size pieces

- ⮑ 2 tablespoons butter

- ⮑ 2 cloves garlic, minced

- ⮑ Salt and black pepper, to taste

- ⮑ Fresh parsley, chopped

Instructions:

1. Preheat your air fryer to 200°C/400°F.

2. In a skillet over medium heat, melt the butter. Add garlic and cook for 1-2 minutes.

3. Add the steak bites to the skillet and cook for 3-4 minutes until browned on all sides.

4. Place the steak bites in the air fryer basket and cook for an additional 2-3 minutes until crispy and cooked to your desired level of doneness.

5. Season with salt and black pepper, and sprinkle with chopped parsley.

6. Serve hot.

Crab Cakes

Ingredients:

- 500 g lump crab meat
- 1/2 cup bread crumbs
- 1/4 cup mayonnaise
- 1 large egg
- 1 tablespoon Dijon mustard
- 1 tablespoon Worcestershire sauce
- 2 tablespoons fresh parsley, chopped
- 1/2 teaspoon Old Bay seasoning
- Salt and black pepper, to taste

Instructions:

1. Preheat your air fryer to 190°C/375°F.

2. In a bowl, mix together all the ingredients until well combined.

3. Shape the mixture into 8-10 crab cakes.

4. Place the crab cakes in the air fryer basket and cook for 10-12 minutes until golden brown and crispy.

5. Serve hot with your favourite dipping sauce.

Air Fryer Lobster Tails

Ingredients:

- 2 lobster tails
- 1 tablespoon butter
- Salt and black pepper, to taste
- Fresh lemon wedges, for serving

Instructions:

1. Preheat your air fryer to 200°C/400°F.

2. Using kitchen scissors, cut the top of each lobster tail and carefully loosen the meat from the shell, leaving it attached at the end.

3. Melt the butter in a small bowl and brush it over the meat.

4. Place the lobster tails in the air fryer basket and cook for 6-8 minutes until the meat is opaque and the shell is red.

5. Season with salt and black pepper and serve with fresh lemon wedges.

Roasted Asparagus with Parmesan

Ingredients:

- 1 bunch of asparagus, tough ends removed

- 1 tbsp olive oil

- Salt and freshly ground black pepper, to taste

- 30g freshly grated Parmesan cheese

- 1 tbsp chopped fresh parsley

Instructions:

1. Preheat your air fryer to 200°C/400°F.

2. In a large bowl, toss the asparagus with the olive oil and season with salt and pepper to taste.

3. Arrange the asparagus in a single layer in the air fryer basket.

4. Air fry the asparagus for 8-10 minutes, shaking the basket occasionally, until tender and lightly browned.

5. Remove the asparagus from the air fryer basket and transfer to a serving platter.

6. Sprinkle the freshly grated Parmesan cheese over the top of the asparagus.

7. Place the platter back in the air fryer and air fry for an additional minute, until the cheese is melted and bubbly.

8. Sprinkle the chopped parsley over the top of the asparagus and serve hot.

9

Vegetarian and Vegan Recipes

Air Fryer Stuffed Mushrooms

Ingredients:

- 8-10 large mushrooms

- 2 tbsp. olive oil

- 1/4 cup chopped onion

- 2 cloves garlic, minced

- 1/4 cup chopped fresh parsley

- 1/4 cup breadcrumbs

- 1/4 cup grated Parmesan cheese

- Salt and pepper to taste

Instructions:

1. Preheat the air fryer to 375°F.

2. Wash and remove the stems from the mushrooms. Finely chop the stems and set them aside.

3. In a skillet over medium heat, sauté the onion, garlic, and chopped mushroom stems in olive oil until softened.

4. Stir in the parsley, breadcrumbs, Parmesan cheese, salt, and pepper.

5. Spoon the filling into each mushroom cap, pressing it down lightly.

6. Place the stuffed mushrooms in the air fryer basket and cook for 8-10 minutes, or until the mushrooms are tender and the filling is golden brown.

7. Serve the stuffed mushrooms hot, garnished with additional parsley if desired.

Air Fryer Falafel

Ingredients:

- 1 can of chickpeas, drained and rinsed

- 1 small onion, chopped

- 1/4 cup fresh parsley, chopped

- 2 cloves of garlic, minced

- 1 tbsp. olive oil

- 1 tbsp. lemon juice

- 1 tsp. ground cumin

- 1/2 tsp. ground coriander

- 1/4 tsp. cayenne pepper

- Salt and pepper to taste

- 1/4 cup all-purpose flour

- Cooking spray

Instructions:

1. Preheat the air fryer to 200°C.

2. In a food processor, pulse the chickpeas, onion, parsley, garlic, olive oil, lemon juice, cumin, coriander, cayenne pepper, salt, and pepper until the mixture becomes a coarse paste.

3. Transfer the mixture to a mixing bowl and stir in the flour until the mixture becomes sticky.

4. Shape the mixture into small balls or patties.

5. Spray the air fryer basket with cooking spray and place the falafel balls or patties in the basket in a single layer.

6. Spray the tops of the falafel with cooking spray.

7. Air fry for 10-12 minutes, or until golden brown and crispy, flipping the falafel halfway through cooking.

8. Serve the falafel hot with hummus, tzatziki, or your favorite sauce.

Vegetable Spring Rolls

Ingredients:

- ⟳ 8 spring roll wrappers

- ⟳ 1 cup shredded cabbage

- ⟳ 1 cup shredded carrots

- ⟳ 1 cup sliced bell peppers

- ⟳ 1 cup sliced mushrooms

- ⟳ 2 tbsp. soy sauce

- ⟳ 1 tbsp. sesame oil

- ⟳ 1 tbsp. rice vinegar

- ⟳ 1 tsp. grated ginger

- ⟳ 1 garlic clove, minced

- ⟳ Cooking spray

Instructions:

1. Preheat the air fryer to 200°C.

2. In a mixing bowl, combine the cabbage, carrots, bell peppers, mushrooms, soy sauce, sesame oil, rice vinegar, ginger, and garlic.

3. Mix well until the vegetables are coated in the sauce.

4. Lay a spring roll wrapper on a flat surface.

5. Spoon some of the vegetable mixture onto the center of the wrapper.

6. Fold the bottom of the wrapper over the vegetables, then fold in the sides, and roll the wrapper tightly to enclose the filling.

7. Repeat with the remaining wrappers and filling.

8. Spray the air fryer basket with cooking spray.

9. Place the spring rolls in the basket in a single layer.

10. Spray the tops of the spring rolls with cooking spray.

11. Air fry for 8-10 minutes, or until golden brown and crispy, flipping the spring rolls halfway through cooking.

12. Serve the spring rolls hot with sweet chili sauce or your favorite dipping sauce.

Veggie Burgers

Ingredients:

- ➲ 1 can of chickpeas, drained and rinsed

- ➲ 1 small onion, chopped

- ➲ 2 cloves of garlic, minced

- ➲ 1 small carrot, grated

- ➲ 1 small zucchini, grated

- ➲ 1/4 cup of breadcrumbs

- ➲ 1/4 cup of flour

- ➲ 1 tsp of cumin

- ➲ 1 tsp of paprika

- ➲ Salt and pepper to taste

- ➲ 1 tbsp of olive oil

Instructions:

1. In a large mixing bowl, add the chickpeas and mash them with a fork or potato masher.

2. Add the chopped onion, minced garlic, grated carrot, and grated zucchini to the mixing bowl.

3. Add the breadcrumbs, flour, cumin, paprika, salt, and pepper to the mixing bowl. Mix all the ingredients together until well combined.

4. Divide the mixture into 4-6 equal portions and form each portion into a patty.

5. Preheat your air fryer to 360°F (180°C) for 5 minutes.

6. Brush each side of the patties with olive oil.

7. Place the patties in the air fryer basket and cook for 10-12 minutes, flipping once halfway through the cooking time.

8. Serve the veggie burgers on buns with your favorite toppings.

Air Fryer Tofu Satay

Ingredients:

- ➲ 1 block of firm tofu, pressed and cut into cubes
- ➲ 1/4 cup of peanut butter
- ➲ 1 tbsp of soy sauce
- ➲ 1 tbsp of maple syrup
- ➲ 1 tbsp of lime juice
- ➲ 1 clove of garlic, minced
- ➲ 1/4 tsp of ginger powder
- ➲ Salt and pepper to taste
- ➲ Skewers

Instructions:

1. In a mixing bowl, whisk together the peanut butter, soy sauce, maple syrup, lime juice, minced garlic, ginger powder, salt, and pepper.

2. Add the cubed tofu to the mixing bowl and gently toss to coat each piece with the sauce.

3. Preheat your air fryer to 400°F (200°C) for 5 minutes.

4. Thread the tofu cubes onto skewers, leaving some space in between each piece.

5. Place the skewers in the air fryer basket and cook for 10-12 minutes, flipping once halfway through the cooking time.

6. Serve the tofu satay skewers with additional peanut sauce for dipping.

Cauliflower Wings

Ingredients:

- 1 small head of cauliflower, cut into bite-sized florets
- 1/2 cup of flour
- 1 tsp of garlic powder
- 1 tsp of paprika
- 1/4 tsp of cayenne pepper
- Salt and pepper to taste
- 1/2 cup of milk
- 1/2 cup of breadcrumbs
- Cooking spray

Instructions:

1. In a mixing bowl, whisk together the flour, garlic powder, paprika, cayenne pepper, salt, and pepper.

2. Add the milk to the mixing bowl and whisk until you have a smooth batter.

3. Place the breadcrumbs in a shallow dish.

4. Dip each cauliflower floret into the batter, shaking off any excess, and then coat it in breadcrumbs.

5. Preheat your air fryer to 400°F (200°C) for 5 minutes.

6. Lightly spray the air fryer basket with cooking spray.

7. Place the cauliflower florets in the air fryer basket in a single layer, leaving some space in between each piece. 8. Cook the cauliflower wings in the air fryer for 10-12 minutes, flipping once halfway through the cooking time, or until they are crispy and golden brown.

8. Repeat the process with any remaining cauliflower florets until they are all cooked.

9. Serve the cauliflower wings with your favorite dipping sauce.

10

International Recipes

Air Fryer Chimichangas

Ingredients:

- 1 lb ground beef

- 1 small onion, chopped

- 1 small bell pepper, chopped

- 2 cloves of garlic, minced

- 1 tbsp of chili powder

- 1 tsp of cumin

- Salt and pepper to taste

- 8 flour tortillas

- 1 cup of shredded cheese

- Cooking spray

Instructions:

1. In a large skillet, cook the ground beef over medium heat until it is browned and cooked through.

2. Add the chopped onion, chopped bell pepper, minced garlic, chili powder, cumin, salt, and pepper to the skillet. Cook until the vegetables are tender.

3. Preheat your air fryer to 400°F (200°C) for 5 minutes.

4. Place a spoonful of the beef mixture and some shredded cheese on each tortilla. Fold the sides in and then roll up each tortilla to form a chimichanga.

5. Spray the chimichangas with cooking spray on both sides.

6. Place the chimichangas in the air fryer basket and cook for 10-12 minutes, flipping once halfway through the cooking time, or until they are crispy and golden brown.

7. Serve the chimichangas with your favorite toppings, such as salsa, guacamole, and sour cream.

Chinese Chicken Wings

Ingredients:

- ➲ 2 lbs of chicken wings
- ➲ 2 tbsp of soy sauce
- ➲ 1 tbsp of hoisin sauce
- ➲ 1 tbsp of honey
- ➲ 1 tbsp of rice vinegar
- ➲ 1 tbsp of sesame oil
- ➲ 1 tsp of garlic powder
- ➲ 1 tsp of ginger powder
- ➲ Salt and pepper to taste
- ➲ Cooking spray
- ➲ Green onions and sesame seeds for garnish

Instructions:

1. In a mixing bowl, whisk together the soy sauce, hoisin sauce, honey, rice vinegar, sesame oil, garlic powder, ginger powder, salt, and pepper.

2. Add the chicken wings to the mixing bowl and toss to coat each wing with the sauce.

3. Preheat your air fryer to 380°F (190°C) for 5 minutes.

4. Spray the air fryer basket with cooking spray.

5. Place the chicken wings in the air fryer basket in a single layer, leaving some space in between each wing.

6. Cook the chicken wings in the air fryer for 12-15 minutes, flipping once halfway through the cooking time, or until they are crispy and cooked through.

7. Garnish the chicken wings with chopped green onions and sesame seeds before serving.

Chicken Shawarma

Ingredients:

- 500 g of boneless, skinless chicken breasts, sliced
- 1 small onion, chopped
- 2 cloves of garlic, minced
- 2 tsp of paprika
- 1 tsp of cumin
- 1/2 tsp of coriander
- 1/4 tsp of cinnamon
- Salt and pepper to taste
- Pita bread, for serving
- Lettuce, tomatoes, and cucumber, for serving
- Tzatziki sauce, for serving

Instructions:

1. In a mixing bowl, whisk together the chopped onion, minced garlic, paprika, cumin, coriander, cinnamon, salt, and pepper.

2. Add the sliced chicken to the mixing bowl and toss to coat each piece with the spice mixture.

3. Preheat your air fryer to 390°F (200°C) for 5 minutes.

4. Place the chicken in the air fryer basket in a single layer, leaving some space in between each piece.

5. Cook the chicken in the air fryer for 12-15 minutes, flipping once halfway through the cooking time, or until it is cooked through and golden brown.

6. Serve the chicken shawarma with warmed pita bread, lettuce, tomatoes, cucumber, and tzatziki sauce.

Fish Tacos

Ingredients:

- 500 g of white fish (such as tilapia or cod), cut into strips

- 1/2 cup of all-purpose flour

- 1/2 tsp of chili powder

- 1/2 tsp of garlic powder

- 1/2 tsp of cumin

- 1/2 tsp of salt

- 1/4 tsp of black pepper

- 2 eggs, beaten

- 1 cup of panko breadcrumbs

- Cooking spray

- Corn tortillas, for serving

- Shredded cabbage, for serving

- Pico de gallo, for serving

Instructions:

1. In a mixing bowl, whisk together the flour, chili powder, garlic powder, cumin, salt, and black pepper.

2. Place the beaten eggs in a shallow dish.

3. Place the panko breadcrumbs in another shallow dish.

4. Preheat your air fryer to 390°F (200°C) for 5 minutes.

5. Dip each fish strip in the flour mixture, then in the beaten eggs, and finally in the panko breadcrumbs.

6. Spray the fish strips with cooking spray on both sides.

7. Place the fish strips in the air fryer basket in a single layer, leaving some space in between each strip.

8. Cook the fish in the air fryer for 8-10 minutes, flipping once halfway through the cooking time, or until it is cooked through and crispy.

9. Warm the corn tortillas in the air fryer for 1-2 minutes.

10. Serve the fish tacos with warmed tortillas, shredded cabbage, and pico de gallo.

Samosas

Ingredients:

- ⮑ 200g plain flour
- ⮑ 1/2 tsp salt
- ⮑ 3 tbsp vegetable oil
- ⮑ 80-100ml water
- ⮑ 2 medium potatoes, peeled and diced
- ⮑ 1/2 onion, finely chopped
- ⮑ 1/2 cup peas
- ⮑ 1 tsp cumin seeds
- ⮑ 1 tsp coriander powder
- ⮑ 1/2 tsp turmeric powder
- ⮑ 1/2 tsp garam masala
- ⮑ 1 green chili, finely chopped (optional)
- ⮑ Salt to taste
- ⮑ 1 tbsp vegetable oil
- ⮑ Cooking spray

Directions:

1. In a mixing bowl, add the flour and salt. Mix well.

2. Add the vegetable oil to the flour mixture and use your fingers to rub it in until the mixture resembles breadcrumbs.

3. Gradually add the water, a little at a time, and mix until a soft and pliable dough is formed. Cover with a damp cloth and set aside.

4. In a frying pan, heat 1 tablespoon of vegetable oil over medium heat.

5. Add the cumin seeds and let them sizzle for a few seconds.

6. Add the onions and sauté until they are translucent.

7. Add the diced potatoes, peas, coriander powder, turmeric powder, garam masala, green chili (if using) and salt. Stir well to combine.

8. Cover the pan and cook for 10-15 minutes, stirring occasionally, until the potatoes are tender.

9. Remove from heat and let the mixture cool completely.

10. Preheat the air fryer to 180°C.

11. Divide the dough into 6 equal portions and roll each portion into a ball.

12. Roll each ball into a thin circle, approximately 15cm in diameter.

13. Cut each circle in half to form two semi-circles.

14. Take one semi-circle and brush the straight edge with water.

15. Form a cone by bringing the straight edge over to form a triangle and pressing the edges together.

16. Fill the cone with 1-2 tablespoons of the potato filling, making sure not to overfill.

17. Brush the open edge of the cone with water and pinch it closed to seal the samosa.

18. Repeat with the remaining dough and filling to make 12 samosas.

19. Lightly spray the samosas with cooking spray and place them in the air fryer.

20. Air fry for 10-12 minutes, until golden brown and crispy.

21. Serve hot with your favourite dipping sauce.

11

Takeaway Inspired Recipes

Air Fryer General Tso's Chicken

Ingredients:

- 500 g boneless, skinless chicken breast, cut into bite-sized pieces
- 1/4 cup cornstarch
- 1/4 cup soy sauce
- 1/4 cup rice vinegar
- 2 tbsp honey
- 1 tbsp hoisin sauce
- 1 tbsp sesame oil
- 1 tbsp grated ginger
- 3 garlic cloves, minced
- 1/4 tsp red pepper flakes
- 1 egg, beaten
- 1/2 cup panko breadcrumbs
- Cooking spray
- Chopped green onions and sesame seeds for garnish

Directions:

1. In a small bowl, whisk together soy sauce, rice vinegar, honey, hoisin sauce, sesame oil, ginger, garlic, and red pepper flakes to make the sauce.

2. In a separate bowl, coat chicken pieces with cornstarch.

3. Dip chicken into beaten egg, then coat with panko breadcrumbs.

4. Preheat the air fryer to 390°F.

5. Lightly spray the air fryer basket with cooking spray.

6. Add chicken to the air fryer basket in a single layer, spraying with cooking spray.

7. Air fry for 8-10 minutes, flipping halfway through, until chicken is cooked through and crispy.

8. Toss chicken in sauce and serve with garnish of chopped green onions and sesame seeds.

Sweet and Sour Pork

Ingredients:

- 500 g pork tenderloin, cut into bite-sized pieces

- 1/4 cup cornstarch

- 1/4 cup soy sauce

- 1/4 cup rice vinegar

- 2 tbsp honey

- 1 tbsp ketchup

- 1 tbsp brown sugar

- 1 tbsp grated ginger

- 3 garlic cloves, minced

- 1/4 cup pineapple juice

- 1/4 cup water

- Cooking spray

- Chopped green onions for garnish

Directions:

1. In a small bowl, whisk together soy sauce, rice vinegar, honey, ketchup, brown sugar, ginger, garlic, pineapple juice, and water to make the sauce.

2. In a separate bowl, coat pork pieces with cornstarch.

3. Preheat the air fryer to 390°F.

4. Lightly spray the air fryer basket with cooking spray.

5. Add pork to the air fryer basket in a single layer, spraying with cooking spray.

6. Air fry for 8-10 minutes, flipping halfway through, until pork is cooked through and crispy.

7. Toss pork in sauce and serve with garnish of chopped green onions.

Air Fryer Orange Chicken

Ingredients:

- 500 g boneless, skinless chicken breast, cut into bite-sized pieces
- 1/4 cup cornstarch
- 1/4 cup soy sauce
- 1/4 cup orange juice
- 2 tbsp honey
- 1 tbsp rice vinegar
- 1 tbsp grated ginger
- 3 garlic cloves, minced
- 1/4 tsp red pepper flakes
- 1 egg, beaten
- 1/2 cup panko breadcrumbs
- Cooking spray
- Orange zest and chopped green onions for garnish

Directions:

1. In a small bowl, whisk together soy sauce, orange juice, honey, rice vinegar, ginger, garlic, and red pepper flakes to make the sauce.

2. In a separate bowl, coat chicken pieces with cornstarch.

3. Dip chicken into beaten egg, then coat with panko breadcrumbs.

4. Preheat the air fryer to 180°C.

5. Lightly spray the air fryer basket with cooking spray.

6. Add chicken to the air fryer basket in a single layer, spraying with cooking spray.

7. Air fry for 8-10 minutes, flipping halfway through, until chicken is cooked through and crispy.

8. Toss chicken in sauce and serve with garnish of orange zest and chopped green onions.

Kung Pao Chicken

Ingredients:

- 500 g boneless, skinless chicken breast, cut into bite-sized pieces

- 1/4 cup cornstarch

- 1/4 cup soy sauce

- 2 tbsp rice vinegar

- 1 tbsp honey

- 1 tbsp hoisin sauce

- 1 tbsp grated ginger

- 3 garlic cloves, minced

- 1/4 tsp red pepper flakes

- 1/2 cup roasted peanuts

- Cooking spray

- Chopped green onions for garnish

Directions:

1. In a small bowl, whisk together soy sauce, rice vinegar, honey, hoisin sauce, ginger, garlic, and red pepper flakes to make the sauce.

2. In a separate bowl, coat chicken pieces with cornstarch.

3. Preheat the air fryer to 180°C.

4. Lightly spray the air fryer basket with cooking spray.

5. Add chicken to the air fryer basket in a single layer, spraying with cooking spray.

6. Air fry for 8-10 minutes, flipping halfway through, until chicken is cooked through and crispy.

7. Toss chicken in sauce and top with roasted peanuts.

8. Serve with garnish of chopped green onions.

Air Fryer Sesame Chicken

Ingredients:

- 500 g boneless, skinless chicken breasts, cut into bite-sized pieces
- 1/4 cup cornstarch
- 1 egg, beaten
- 1/2 cup panko breadcrumbs
- Cooking spray
- Salt and pepper to taste
- 2 tbsp soy sauce
- 2 tbsp honey
- 1 tbsp rice vinegar
- 1 tsp sesame oil
- 1 garlic clove, minced
- 1 tsp grated ginger
- 1 tbsp cornstarch mixed with 1 tbsp water
- 2 tbsp sesame seeds
- Sliced green onions for garnish

Directions:

1. Preheat the air fryer to 180°C.

2. In a shallow bowl, coat chicken pieces with cornstarch.

3. Dip chicken into beaten egg, then coat with panko breadcrumbs.

4. Lightly spray the air fryer basket with cooking spray.

5. Add chicken to the air fryer basket in a single layer, spraying with cooking spray.

6. Air fry for 12-15 minutes, flipping halfway through, until chicken is cooked through and crispy.

7. In a small saucepan, whisk together soy sauce, honey, rice vinegar, sesame oil, garlic, and ginger.

8. Heat the saucepan over medium heat and bring the mixture to a simmer.

9. Stir in cornstarch mixture and cook for 1-2 minutes, until the sauce thickens.

10. Remove the chicken from the air fryer basket and toss with the sesame sauce.

11. Sprinkle sesame seeds over the chicken and serve with sliced green onions. Enjoy!

12

Air Fryer Sandwiches

Air Fryer Turkey Club

Ingredients:

- 6 slices turkey breast

- 6 slices bacon

- 4 slices bread

- 4 lettuce leaves

- 4 tomato slices

- 4 slices cheese

- 2 tbsp mayonnaise

- Salt and pepper to taste

- Cooking spray

Directions:

1. Preheat the air fryer to 180°C.

2. Lay bacon in the air fryer basket in a single layer.

3. Air fry for 8-10 minutes, flipping halfway through, until bacon is crispy. Remove from the air fryer and set aside.

4.   Lightly spray the air fryer basket with cooking spray.

5.   Toast bread slices in the air fryer for 1-2 minutes, until lightly golden.

6.   Assemble the sandwich by spreading mayonnaise on one side of each toast slice.

7.   On one slice, layer turkey, bacon, lettuce, tomato, and cheese.

8.   Top with the other slice of bread, mayonnaise side down.

9.   Place the sandwich in the air fryer basket and air fry for 3-5 minutes, until cheese is melted and bread is toasted to your desired level of crispiness.

10. Remove from the air fryer basket and cut in half.

11. Serve hot and enjoy your delicious Air Fryer Turkey Club sandwich!

Philly Cheesesteak Sandwich

Ingredients:

- 500 g ribeye steak, thinly sliced

- 1/2 green bell pepper, thinly sliced

- 1/2 onion, thinly sliced

- 4 slices provolone cheese

- 4 hoagie rolls

- 2 tbsp butter

- Salt and pepper to taste

- Cooking spray

Directions:

1. Preheat the air fryer to 200°C.

2. Lightly spray the air fryer basket with cooking spray.

3. In a skillet over medium-high heat, cook steak until browned, about 2-3 minutes per side. Remove from the skillet and set aside.

4. In the same skillet, melt butter and sauté bell pepper and onion until softened and slightly caramelized, about 5-7 minutes.

5. Add steak to the skillet and toss with the vegetables. Season with salt and pepper to taste.

6. Split hoagie rolls in half and lightly toast them in the air fryer for 1-2 minutes.

7. Divide the steak and vegetable mixture among the rolls.

8. Top each sandwich with a slice of provolone cheese.

9. Place the sandwiches in the air fryer basket and air fry for 1-2 minutes, until cheese is melted and bread is crispy.

10. Serve hot and enjoy your delicious Philly Cheesesteak Sandwich!

Pulled Pork Sandwich

Ingredients:

- ➲ 500 g pork shoulder, trimmed and cut into 2-inch cubes

- ➲ 1/2 cup barbecue sauce

- ➲ 4 hamburger buns

- ➲ 4 slices cheddar cheese

- ➲ 1/4 cup coleslaw

- ➲ Salt and pepper to taste

- ➲ Cooking spray

Directions:

1. Preheat the air fryer to 180°C.

2. Lightly spray the air fryer basket with cooking spray.

3. Season pork shoulder with salt and pepper.

4. Add pork shoulder to the air fryer basket and air fry for 20-25 minutes, until cooked through and tender.

5. Shred the pork shoulder with a fork.

6. In a small saucepan, heat barbecue sauce over medium heat.

7. Toast hamburger buns in the air fryer for 1-2 minutes, until lightly golden.

8. Assemble the sandwich by placing pulled pork on the bottom half of each bun.

9. Top each sandwich with a slice of cheddar cheese.

10. Drizzle barbecue sauce over the cheese.

11. Top with coleslaw.

12. Close the sandwiches and place them in the air fryer basket.

13. Air fry for 1-2 minutes, until cheese is melted and bread is crispy.

14. Remove from the air fryer basket and cut in half.

15. Serve hot and enjoy your delicious Pulled Pork Sandwich!

13

Air Fryer Appetizers for Parties

Buffalo Chicken Dip

Ingredients:

- 2 cups shredded chicken
- 1/2 cup buffalo sauce
- 1/2 cup ranch dressing
- 1/2 cup cream cheese, softened
- 1/2 cup sour cream
- 1/2 cup shredded cheddar cheese
- Salt and pepper to taste
- Cooking spray

Directions:

1. Preheat the air fryer to 180°C.

2. Lightly spray a baking dish with cooking spray.

3. In a mixing bowl, combine shredded chicken, buffalo sauce, ranch dressing, cream cheese, and sour cream.

4. Season with salt and pepper to taste.

5. Spread the mixture in the baking dish.

6. Top with shredded cheddar cheese.

7. Place the dish in the air fryer basket and air fry for 8-10 minutes, until cheese is melted and bubbly.

8. Remove from the air fryer basket and serve hot with tortilla chips or crackers.

Jalapeno Poppers

Ingredients:

- 12 jalapeno peppers, halved and seeded
- 100g cream cheese, softened
- 1/2 cup shredded cheddar cheese
- 1/2 cup breadcrumbs
- 1/2 tsp garlic powder
- 1/2 tsp paprika
- Salt and pepper to taste
- Cooking spray

Directions:

1. Preheat the air fryer to 180°C.
2. Lightly spray the air fryer basket with cooking spray.
3. In a mixing bowl, combine cream cheese, cheddar cheese, breadcrumbs, garlic powder, paprika, salt, and pepper.
4. Mix well until fully combined.

5. Stuff each jalapeno half with the cheese mixture.

6. Place the jalapeno poppers in the air fryer basket and air fry for 6-8 minutes, until golden and crispy.

7. Remove from the air fryer basket and serve hot.

Loaded Potato Skins

Ingredients:

- ➲ 4 medium potatoes
- ➲ 1/2 cup shredded cheddar cheese
- ➲ 4 slices bacon, cooked and crumbled
- ➲ 1/4 cup sour cream
- ➲ 2 tbsp chopped chives
- ➲ Salt and pepper to taste
- ➲ Cooking spray

Directions:

1. Preheat the air fryer to 180°C.

2. Lightly spray the air fryer basket with cooking spray.

3. Pierce each potato with a fork several times.

4. Place potatoes in the air fryer basket and air fry for 25-30 minutes, until cooked through and tender.

5. Let potatoes cool slightly, then cut them in half lengthwise.

6. Scoop out the flesh of each potato half, leaving a thin layer on the skin.

7. In a mixing bowl, combine potato flesh, cheddar cheese, bacon, sour cream, chives, salt, and pepper.

8. Mix well until fully combined.

9. Stuff each potato skin half with the potato mixture.

10. Place the potato skins in the air fryer basket and air fry for 6-8 minutes, until golden and crispy.

11. Remove from the air fryer basket and serve hot.

Meatballs

Ingredients:

- ⮌ 500g ground beef
- ⮌ 1/2 cup breadcrumbs
- ⮌ 1/4 cup grated Parmesan cheese
- ⮌ 1/4 cup milk
- ⮌ 1 egg
- ⮌ 2 cloves garlic, minced
- ⮌ 1 tsp dried oregano
- ⮌ Salt and pepper to taste
- ⮌ Cooking spray

Directions:

1. Preheat the air fryer to 180°C.

2. Lightly spray the air fryer with cooking spray

3. In a mixing bowl, combine ground beef, breadcrumbs, Parmesan cheese, milk, egg, garlic, oregano, salt, and pepper.

4. Mix well until fully combined.

5. Form the mixture into small meatballs, about 1 inch in diameter.

6. Place the meatballs in the air fryer basket and air fry for 10-12 minutes, until cooked through and browned.

7. Remove from the air fryer basket and serve hot with your favorite dipping sauce.

Fried Pickles

Ingredients:

- 1 cup dill pickle slices

- 1/2 cup flour

- 1/2 cup breadcrumbs

- 1/2 tsp garlic powder

- 1/2 tsp paprika

- 1/4 tsp cayenne pepper

- Salt and pepper to taste

- 1 egg, beaten

- Cooking spray

Directions:

1. Preheat the air fryer to 375°F.

2. Lightly spray the air fryer basket with cooking spray.

3. In a shallow dish, combine flour, breadcrumbs, garlic powder, paprika, cayenne pepper, salt, and pepper.

4. In another shallow dish, beat the egg.

5. Dip each pickle slice into the beaten egg, then coat with the breadcrumb mixture.

6. Place the pickle slices in the air fryer basket and air fry for 6-8 minutes, until golden and crispy.

7. Remove from the air fryer basket and serve hot with your favorite dipping sauce.

Mac and Cheese Bites

Ingredients:

- ⮑ 1 cup elbow macaroni (cooked and drained)
- ⮑ 1 tbsp unsalted butter
- ⮑ 1 tbsp all-purpose flour
- ⮑ 1/2 cup whole milk
- ⮑ 1/2 tsp salt
- ⮑ 1/4 tsp black pepper
- ⮑ 1/2 tsp garlic powder
- ⮑ 1/2 tsp onion powder
- ⮑ 1/2 cup shredded cheddar cheese
- ⮑ 1/2 cup panko bread crumbs
- ⮑ 1 egg (beaten)

Instructions:

1. In a medium saucepan, melt butter over medium heat.

2. Add flour and whisk to combine. Cook for 1-2 minutes.

3. Slowly pour in the milk while whisking continuously.

4. Cook the mixture for 2-3 minutes, stirring frequently until it thickens.

5. Add the cooked macaroni to the saucepan and stir to combine.

6. Add salt, black pepper, garlic powder, onion powder and cheddar cheese. Stir until cheese is melted.

7. Pour the mac and cheese mixture into a baking dish and chill in the fridge for at least 1 hour.

8. Preheat the air fryer to 400°F (200°C).

9. Using a cookie scoop or spoon, form mac and cheese mixture into small bite-size balls.

10. Dip each ball into the beaten egg and then coat with panko bread crumbs.

11. Spray the air fryer basket with cooking spray.

12. Place the mac and cheese bites in the air fryer basket, and air fry for 8-10 minutes, or until golden and crispy.

13. Remove from the air fryer and serve hot.

Onion Rings

Ingredients:

- ⮕ 2 large onions

- ⮕ 1/2 cup all-purpose flour

- ⮕ 1/2 tsp paprika

- ⮕ 1/2 tsp salt

- ⮕ 1/4 tsp black pepper

- ⮕ 1 egg

- ⮕ 1/2 cup milk

- ⮕ 1 cup panko bread crumbs

Instructions:

1. Preheat the air fryer to 400°F (200°C).

2. Cut onions into 1/2 inch thick slices and separate them into rings.

3. In a shallow dish, whisk together flour, paprika, salt, and black pepper.

4. In another shallow dish, whisk together egg and milk.

5. Place panko bread crumbs in a third shallow dish.

6. Dip each onion ring into the flour mixture, then the egg mixture, and finally the bread crumbs.

7. Lightly spray the air fryer basket with cooking spray.

8. Place the onion rings in the air fryer basket in a single layer.

9. Air fry for 10-12 minutes or until golden and crispy, flipping halfway through.

10. Remove from the air fryer and serve hot.

Printed in Great Britain
by Amazon